GARDENING IN THE DARK

GARDENING
in the DARK

Laura Kasischke

AUSABLE PRESS
2004

Cover art: "Dancing Flowers" (x-ray)
by Bryan Whitney
Design and composition by Ausable Press
The type is Palatino.
Cover design by Rebecca Soderholm

Published by
AUSABLE PRESS
1026 HURRICANE ROAD, KEENE NY 12942
www.ausablepress.org

Distributed to the trade by:
CONSORTIUM BOOK SALES & DISTRIBUTION
1045 WESTGATE DRIVE
SAINT PAUL, MN 55114-1065
(651) 221-9035
(651) 221-0124 (fax)
(800) 283-3572 (orders)

The acknowledgments appear on page 97 and constitute
a continuation of the copyrights page.

Library of Congress Cataloging-in-Publication Data
Kasischke, Laura 1961—
Gardening in the dark / Laura Kasischke.--1st ed.
p. cm.
ISBN 1-931337-22-5 (pbk. : alk. paper)
I. Title.

PS3561.A6993G37 2004
811'.54--dc22
2004005572

for B.A. & J.A.

There were three ravens sat on a tree,
And they were black as they might be.
The one of them said to his make,
"Where shall we our breakfast take?"

—*"The Three Ravens"*

She, supposing him to be the gardener,
saith unto him . . .

—*John 20: 15*

GARDENING IN THE DARK

I.

II.

I.

CHILDHOOD FRIEND

Is this what you asked for, my friend, these words, is
        this
what you meant when you said—?

On the bus, it settled between us, the dead
skin of living

children in a blizzard. Sand
from the stars. Ancient violets. The crushed

wings of bees and the dander of birds. So
much small stuff, yes, on the breeze, but at our desks
        the sun

made a circus of it. Asthma, weeping, elephants,
and clowns. A man slipped screaming from his trapeze

as a sequined girl twirled
over him in a noose—

Excuse me? I couldn't
hear what you said

over the roar of the billion
specks descending, over the accumulation of flakes
        and scales.

You asked me for something, I know that much, I know
you called my name

as you stumbled down the garden
path beneath my bed, gasping, as you knelt down there

and died
among the childhood flowers made of dust and human
        hair.

BLACK DRESS

I could go no further than that first line:
Spring comes even to the closet.
The words like little iron blossoms on a vine.

The parks full of people under a heathery sky.
The music of silverware, of violins.
Near the road, a woman paints
the pickets of her fence with blinding light.

When Herod sat down at the dinner table, the roasted
bird flew from the platter crying, "Christ lives! He is
    alive!"
It's spring, even at night.
The mushrooms damply reflect the stars.
All manner of pale flesh, opened up like eyes. Moon-
    light

on the jellyfish. In the dark
grass the startling muteness of a child's
white rubber rat.

But the closet. Even

in spring, the closet's a blind hive. A black dress

hangs at its center—like Persephone, it's

the closet's prisoner,
and its queen. *Never forget,*
it sings. *I saw you then. I saw it all:*

After the funeral, the riotous dance. After the wedding,
     the long

weeping and kneeling in the bathroom stall.

Oh, there are birds the world's
entirely forgotten (winter, amnesia) singing again
to the comings and the goings, the bright

and empty flashes,
the openings and closings. *Sweetheart,*
I'm leaving. Honey, I'm home. But that

black dress hangs always and omniscient in its single
     thought, its

accumulating mass—a darkness
tucked into another darkness:
where I wore it first,

where I'll wear it last.

CLOCK RADIO

Such easy sleep.
A simple eloquence.
Like a sail cutting a clean
incision through the breeze.
Yards and yards of white sky.
The laundering instructions on my sheets:

Machine wash warm. Tumble dry.

The traffic was made out of silence.
The meters had all expired.
An abandoned sand-bag factory

brooded on a hillside. It was

all a child's drawing, a whole
world made out of paper and a single straight line.
I could have heard the tip of a too-sharp pencil snap

under the slightest pressure, but this

was a ship full of virgins crossing
a placid ocean together,
singing a song
lost between two stations.
Nothing was ever less likely to wake me.

No, I was the cat curled
into the corner
having just torn to pieces and eaten
the brightest-voiced bird in the world.

Turned it to purring and sun. That

was the music of the morning, a soft

storm of feathers, a couple
tablespoons of blood,
and, at the center, the slightest pulse.

I slept until late afternoon.

No, I slept forever.

ALCOHOLISM

It had nothing to do with how much they drank:

How much they drank!
The Christmas tree lit like a ladder on fire.
The heart like a kerosene lamp.

In France, a little dog
who could dance the minuet.
In Vienna, a deaf man writing symphonies in an attic.

Strange things happened in our house
the hour after happy hour. Call

that one the Hour
of the Tender Parent, Hour of the Big Happy Plan.
Love and tears and bravado, and a patience
like dust settling on a slab

of marble
in a cathedral
in a small medieval town, a town

in which our ancestors
laughed, passing a flask.

That was the flask in which I was conceived.
The test-tube the world was made in.

A blue vapor rose
swirling from its throat, a thin
veil that became the cosmos.

And somewhere, a linear accelerator, waiting.
An atomic number assigned
to every one of us.

This homeland, a prologue.
This country with no king

except its mercurial soul. Its spirit. Its tincture.
Somewhere . . . stars, sex, libraries, and that
music I'd been waiting
all my life to hear. Where
was Bach before he reached my ears?

Bach, in the half-finished basement.
Beethoven in the snow at the television's borders.

A beggar somewhere found
a ten-dollar bill in the street.
O, Bach

was everywhere I didn't listen.
At the bottom of the fountain at the center of the mall—
all those shiny coins, I could
have dipped my hands right in
if I hadn't been afraid to get caught.

And the forests, full of evergreen!
Moss and pine and the canned scent of spring.

They were perfectly happy
for a long, long time. When I
close my eyes I can see them still
wearing the fabric my memory is made of—

inexpensive, easy to clean.
They were everything to me

in their plaid clothes
on our plaid couch.

HAPPY MEAL
for Jack

At the bottom of the bag, there is a fact
(a bit of joy, a bit of junk) which my son was issued

from the womb into this world knowing.

All those years, the way we lived!
So much gardening in the dark.
Or an old blind woman sewing
a tremulous rose on a tablecloth. *Have*

a great night, the boy
at the second drive-thru window says. He smiles

like a boy who woke
only moments ago
to the sound of a moth
in a city made of linen.

Autumn already, and the showy
flowers are over, retreated
into the earth. It simply

means what it is:
Neither beginning
nor *fin de siecle*

regardless of the way it feels. Unlike

the child in the carseat behind me, I'm old
enough to remember
when the television used to sign off.
The star-spangled banner
and a flag in the wind
followed by nothing but fuzz. How

many nights
I woke to that fuzz, a girl
in the center of a dress
made of electrical dust.

For years, I watched the news, and still
I saw this world
as through a shower door, steamily, and taught
my child to speak
of the griefs of the past
in silly words and song:

Boo-boo, ashes, we all fall down. But

once a father bolted his doors and said to his family, *We*
must allow our friends and neighbors
to call on us no more.

It is a little monster, this fact
at the bottom of the bag, this complimentary toy.
And to the child behind me, it seems
completely free, despite the price. O Happy Meal: even
        happier, the *happiest*

meal of our lives! No
end of the world. No horizon on fire.
And a blessing before I forget:

May some beautiful evening in the future find you

sipping wine with your beloved
in a peaceful foreign country

while the lake moves full of shredded moon
and tiny candle-lit fish,

and the sound of a violin
played expertly in another room

and my death, if it has come, not troubling you a bit.

INSCRIPTIONS ON WAX TABLETS

Spring Break

I'm sixteen in the Bahamas. A drunk girl
on a balcony in a sundress
with a pina colada.
Burning, I'm about

to slip out of my own memory altogether—

still dancing, however, still
talking nonsense to a stranger in a salmon-
pink suit according to my friends.

Memory, like a shoebox full of ocean.
This life, like the forgotten plot of a novel:

Oh, the protagonist wakes up early. She grows older.

But through it all, this body also, full of blood and
        thought.
This body, a heavy bubble.

And, under me, a little net
my mother sewed for me
out of naiveté and luck.

Dream

He's back. The death was faked. Yes,
he jumped from the plane, okay, but he had a parachute,
    and now

we're drinking scotch in his motel room, and I'm afraid.
    It's summer

and the sky is full of swaying lamps
and distant planets. I don't want to be alone, but neither

do I wish to be a memory in a motel room in a dead
    man's head.

Party

I misplaced the invitation, and forgot to go, but that
        night
from my bed
I thought I heard the sound
of ice in glasses, dropped
by silver tongs. I looked outside. In the sky,
a few bears and vultures
had become constellations. A few
stories there, a few
more things in this life
I'd almost entirely forgotten. I woke again
when I

heard my name
briefly on the lips of a hostess miles away, remembering

suddenly where I was, and where I wasn't.

Spring Break

Later, the football coach's son
will carry me to bed
and leave me there, untouched. I'll wake up

with one arm flung into my suitcase, and the other
covering my head.

I had been wandering in a staticky meadow
for a long time gathering
intangible flowers and humming
a single note—or so it seemed

until someone showed me a photo:

There I was, indisputably, in the corner, neither

myself nor anyone else, sixteen
in the Bahamas
sipping a pina colada, and tottering

at the edge of a balcony, while
below me that airy net
blew around in the breeze. I'd

never be able to remember a thing, but my

friends would swear I danced all night
with the same guy (pink
suit, my arms around his neck)
and that, after he left, I

lay laughing for a long time
on the damp lawn while
the world

made of danger, made of weight,
spun on without me
and despite me
for someone else's sake.

SACRED FLOWER WATCHING ME

Deep in the ground, in the center
of a bulb, in the scarlet
darkness wrapped in crackling

there is a pinprick
of light. It's hot. It stirs. It's spring—
pitiful and sweet as a small girl spanked.

My love, all of it, a life of it, has been
too little. Nor has my rage ever forced any diamonds
out of the blood through the skin.

How awful
resurrection
for someone like me will be. The teenage
girls are being dragged

out of the earth by their hair.

Tongues, testicles, plums, and small hearts bloat
sweetly in the trees. And then

a silence like water
poured into honey—

the silence of middle age.

But there are nights I feel a sacred
flower watching me.
Such affection!
Even in my cradle, it was waiting
warmly, its soft

white gaze

steady on my insufficient face.

SPEEDING TICKET

The officer asks if I know
why it is I've been pulled over. Oh,
no, I say, not

that armed robbery back in '88? It is a joke

only a woman with two
children in the car, a woman
of a certain age could make. There's a small

pleasant birthmark shaped
like an island I've been to on his face.
I show him the proper papers. Yes,

I've been to that place,
and I know about narrow escapes—so

many sputtering coals
tossed into the mossy shadows among
the forget-me-nots, the violets, the wild oregano.

In a hurry, ma'am, today?

Hell no.
We could have been early
or late. Who cared? They never unlock that gate. What
difference would it make?
What I was after was just
a graceful passage to another place,
and now I know there's no such thing.

A flock of swans
risen from the lake.

No swans. No way.
The self, contrary
to popular opinion, is *not*

the thing that remains. We are
infinite, and it isn't
a question, is it,
of whether or not we could be replaced. Who

among the millions of us
would be worth the trouble it would take?

Truly, I wanted only
to *appear* to obtain such grace, and then

through the years somehow I became
a high brick wall fully expecting
the little blue flowers to thrive in my shade.

Once, I let a crescent wrench
rust for years in snow and rain. I knew

exactly where I'd dropped it, could
have taken you to the high
grass into which I'd let it slip, but there it stayed

until I saw the paperboy pick it up
and put it in his pocket one day.
Strange, only
the other morning
my son said he wanted
to be a policeman, or a demon, when he grew up.
To get bad people, he said.

And I said yes, and I poured more
coffee into my cup, and I

remembered the signs, that the signs
were posted all over that place:

Thin Ice, *No Skating.*

We skated anyway.

The yellow tape.
The psychology majors.
The structuralists, the policy-makers. And how,
when the time finally came
to stand before them and try to explain,

I had nothing at all to say.

Only to find myself suddenly unable
any longer not to say it, finally

having you
here like this, all
ears and leaning
into my window with an island on your face.

True enough, I was not yet naked.
Comprehensive collision, the neighborhood was safe.

I had an address in it, and a name. Only

to find you
this patient beside
my motor vehicle in your final disguise, all
merciless kindness, laughing a little, with a boy's
turquoise eyes.

A voice says *Hurry, I'm burning.*
A voice says *Where are you hurt?*

All those years, I thought
if only there were a fine, I could pay it
wholly, and this slow torture would be over!

A voice says *This
isn't the end,
you know, no
monologue can save you.*
A voice says, *Yes, Officer, I know*

why it is I've been pulled over,

while you write it down,
as I always knew you would.
This gentle reckoning,
all my life,

I was driving toward it as fast as I could.

GINGERBREAD

Dear God, the things I've been—

soldiers, and angels, and stars, and once
some old couple's mortal burden
leaping from an oven.
I've run through snowy fields (blind girl, pine cone)
chased by bears, only to wake
lonely in Paradise, son

of fortunate coincidence and a crone.

The dogs
howled. Someone recited
ominous verses to a child.
My whole life

the worst and best
of everything I've done

has been the business of someone else.
Though I lived for a while in a fancy house
made out of nothing but me, what
was I but

the compulsion of another? A wish

unhinged? A simple reaction
to a simple stimulus?
Neither sweet, nor bitter, nor voluntary.

Given all the causes, all that happened
between aye and nay, night and day—
who would not have been me?

It's one of the inevitable sorrows

stirred by the telling of a story
or the singing of a song.
It's true, the wise and good
do perform heroic acts, but

when something contrary to wisdom or goodness is
        done,
that's an act of fate. I ran

but I was chased.

SUMMER, HERE

In the beginning, the unbelievable burgeoning.
Did I *plant* these things in the garden?
What in God's name are they?

In the beginning . . .
Electricity turned to flesh. A billion
nerves softened and shocked into blossom, slopped

with a big brush
hastily onto the green
velvet curtain we called spring. This

is what happens when the living gets easy. Out
of the moss, a lot of little fingers
digging themselves up. Ah!

such marriage weather,
but in it, too, the delicious
mysteries of some other

couple's precipitous divorce. What

was all that love
but a lot of grasshoppers dancing
in a crate with some overripe plums? *We all*

saw it coming.

"Go ahead," is all my son
wants to hear me say. "Feel
free to jump on the beds today. Flap

your arms and scream
for hours at the top of your lungs."
And my step-daughter, "Hey,

how about I take
you and all your friends to the mall,
and pick you up in seven hours? First

I'd like to give you
two hundred dollars."

And why not? What

a morsel, if you could slip
the bones from a hummingbird and dip
the whole thing in chocolate sauce. What

was so wrong
about the 'seventies? The Free Love, big shoes, *High
Times*, daisy decals
on the shower doors? Now
and then, a few
sober words about death:

Hey, kids, don't play with matches.

But then something changed. The states

make perfect puzzle pieces, like the decades,
like the seasons, but in truth

you can find yourself crossing
from Indiana to Kentucky
without ever knowing you did. The child-

raccoon we fed those bagels to
in the backyard yesterday
is swarmed with black-flies in the road today. See

how neatly God has trained
(with whips and chains) those butterflies
to dance from flower to flower. A few
delicate shreds of terror
trembling in the air.

"I am summer, here

to please you," the world says to me. I nod
pleasantly, but don't forget
the feeling that spread
just under my skin

the day a woman I'd always liked
stopped me in the stairwell to tell me
what she'd always hated about me
as if it were advice.

HARDWARE STORE IN A TOWN
WITHOUT MEN

I found myself in a story
without suspense, only
one deaf falcon circling deafly, and that
wild college girl next door

screaming at her mother on the phone.

My heart, a golden lobster, a star
in a grave, some
hot blood running underground . . .

and all my early daydreams loosed
like termites in the walls
of some deserted church.

Oh, I recognized my agony right away.
The howling dog of daylight life, the years of lust
had opened up
a permanent inn for phantoms in my brain.

Then, I turned forty.
Every morning,

sweeping out the shadows
from the cobwebbed corners, raking
the leaves from the gutters,
the hair from the drains . . .

And sleep, the sweet
rolling water of its e's.
A stroll through the beautiful
ruins of my own dreams.
A hardware store
in a town without men. Whole

shelves devoted to wrenches, gleaming,

and no reason
to lock the door.

No door.

QUIET

All morning I try to kill a fly in the kitchen,
but it isn't ready to die. Who

is? Outside, the vegetable siren. The sky
has folded corners
like a military hat.

Except for the bump and buzz, the house is quiet.
They're all gone. The house
is a thought with a fly inside it, or

a French dreamer
on a hillside . . .

. . . I recall

a boy tapping his pencil on the table
all through Study Hall.
I tried to catch his eye,
and when I couldn't
I reached into myself and pulled
a shadow made of substance
up & over my mind. Like

drowning in a fountain—it was
my watery shroud of language and desire, and I

drank disastrously from it for the rest of my life.

When it comes to nothingness, there is no cup.

I remember my personal prison of sunlight and dust

made on the linoleum by the Venetian blinds.

I remember the joy and the terror of finding

a way to hide
so that no tapping boy could ever again
tap his own existence into mine.

The house this morning is a fly
with a thought inside it,
not wanting to die . . .

The dreamers do not want to wake, but
the documentary makers
are on the way . . .

They are digging up the terracotta soldiers

the emperor ordered for his grave. They

are scattering Ted Bundy's ashes
all over the Cascades from a plane.

THE SORROWS OF CARRIE M.

I was a tower of fury and glory.
They called me Carrie.
A postman's daughter.

The wallpaper, nautical.
The carpet, shag.
I woke in the middle of a story
about myself

without a beginning or an end.
It was nap-time, they said . . .

Oh, the coquelicot is a flower
which does not keep its petals
or promises very well.
My grandfather had the hand of a seabird,

and with it he clutched
the rail of his bed. *Tell*
your grandmother I still love her, he said. So, this is death.

And the boy on the corner: DON'T WALK, the flashing
halo spelled above his head.

But the sky was a blinding cookie sheet on fire.
My mother had such blue eyes!
And my father in his blue shirts, smelling of her iron.

Some evenings over silverware and meat
my parents stared at me:

Carrie, tower
of fury and glory.
I was their only child.

And then my mother died.

The pastel soaps in the soap dish had lied.
There was a teacher poised at a blackboard holding
a piece of yellow chalk.

The teacher was death. The blackboard was the sky.

Oh, my teenage heart a little tear-drenched pillow

                a pin-cushion without pins

                a souvenir from a place
                I wished I'd never been . . .

Oh, the coquelicot is a flower
which doesn't keep its petals
or promises very well.
The soldiers in their bloody boots.
The defoliating breeze.

This was the nineteen-seventies.
Haunted orange, and a whole
false corpus revolved above the dance floor . . .

"Who cares? Who cares?"the sparrow sang to the
    storm . . .

I care, I said. My name is Carrie. I wrote
a letter to the president asking
him to end the war, and then—

One of those carnival games
any child can win. It
had nothing to do with luck. Simply pick a duck—

Got a job at a convenience store.
On the radio, the cynics
sang about love in a chorus. The shadows
of burnt rubber
on a road headed north.

Feebly, those shadows
spoke feebly to me:
Get yourself a man.
So I went out and got one
with muscles and a gun.

Above the house, a black balloon
drifted slowly toward the sun,
and suddenly I wondered—

Where have they gone, those girlhood friends I loved—?

O, Margaret of the scarves. O, gentle-haired Clarisse.

Impaled somewhere on spearmint leaves?

I e-mail them, but I
don't think they'll e-mail me.
Another summer, and I'm stunned
to find myself attached, still, to one
of the sources of this life,

but I don't know which one . . .
Wisdom, beauty, lust . . . ?
While, next door, two teenage boys
speak seriously of amps and lead guitars. But I

know who they are and what they've done.

FORTIETH BIRTHDAY

The night's a nostalgic tablecloth embroidered awk-
wardly with stars:

An animal outside of its skin, what is it?

*If someone offers you a gift, and you refuse it, to whom does
    it belong?*

I want to give advice!
I say to the couple ahead of me in line, "I couldn't
help but overhear—"

And then it begins,
a cold rain,
grayer than champagne.

A toast to the yes-man!
A toast to the nay-sayer!
both of whom I've been.

In the mirror, I'm a woman
who has yet to make the acquaintance
of the woman she is. Which

one of us gets the infinites, which one the vistas: the one
I am, or the one I've been?

Which one the synchronized swimmer, and which

will I be holding the heart when the skin's
been utterly unzipped?—(its
left ventricle spitting
fire, a blue stream of anti-freeze
issuing from the right.)

Is this what *maturity* is?—the sense

of having been
detained at the station
long after I've already boarded the train?

My image
in the mirror
is invisible,

a breath stitched
to a silk slip
in a moment of aloneness. "That's all!"
I hear a woman in the hallway holler.

That's it? This blip?

But what a blip! All

those seconds and minutes zithered into
a million brilliant bits and slivers, stuffed

into a trunk
weighing more than a ton,
and hauled through this life
for forty years

on the back of a butterfly.

YOUNGER WOMAN SHOPPING
FOR A BLOUSE

She holds it up to see it better,
trying to imagine . . .

Where did that last decade go?
I remember

driving fast past
the sloppy needlepoint
of lilacs in the breeze,
dancing in a pine-paneled bar.
I remember

sending a postcard to a man
I'd read about in the paper.
He'd survived an ordeal, but what

was it, and who are you? All

this honey all over my hands.
Where did it come from, and what
if a bear crosses my path now?
What if the bees find me?

She cannot imagine herself
in that, and puts it back.

BLIZZARD AT THE CHELSEA FAIR

Too late I decide I would chase him through the
        gate, un-
strap him from that contraption
and pull him back,

but it's already begun,

the fans and the lights, the whole
thing rising from its platform, and by god,
"She's a Brick House" being sung
sotto voce from the great beyond. Still

for a minute, watching
the rickety thrill of their Blizzard
I would be happiest woman who ever lived
if my son weren't in it.

Then, I catch a glimpse
of him blur by
with what appears to be a smile—little
molecular smear
going somewhere, already been.
But when
I try to wave at him I find

I'm frozen in time,

and also I'm
an entire flock of birds being
buffeted wildly around in the wind. I have

avoided disastrous statistics
all my life until this minute. More

than once, the shadow
of some enormous machine
has rolled right over me,
and I always walked away unscathed. God,

the sloppy temporary jobs I've done, the promises
broken blithely, the revealing
dress I wore

to the funeral of my mother. Satan
winks at me. He knows
I'm thinking, *Give*

me back my boy
and for whatever it's worth
you can have my soul.

"Mom," he says,
touching my shoulder
when the whole thing's over, "There's
something on your skin."

I have yet to decide if it's tears,
or sweat, or blood, or just more skin
when he says, "Mom, I want to go again."

JANUARY

The howling pretends to bring on winter,

but the howling was there all along.

In the miniature roses, in the tiny bees,

in the glittering bits of whatever that was
we called the wind when it was spring:

(Oh, remember, Sweetheart, we called it *breeze*.)

II.

THE ACCIDENT

It was spring, as if a bride
had been bewitched into windchimes. Somewhere
a child

rowed himself in a life jacket
merrily down a stream. The soft

ivory tapping of piano keys in a dream,
while a mother hummed
behind a window screen,
and a breeze gathered itself together so
skillfully in a cherry tree
that it became the last
thing you ever imagined

could happen to you, or *because* of you,
in a billion years, in the blink of an eye. A girl

in an emerald dress unzipped her purse, from which
a swarm of surprised cries issued. It

undulated, a shimmering
tissue on the breeze, a scrap
of crushed light billowing

out of the pineal gland,
out of the parietal lobe,
out of the thyroid and its quiet twilight, and then

it settled on the grass, and you became
that which you could never have imagined

happening, as it happened.

PROTRACTED ABSENCE

Christ so many little gnats, I thought
they were ashes, or eyelashes, traveling
in a cloud the size
and shape of a mind, tossing

themselves into the candle's flame
then settling like a ghastly
snow on the cool
wrinkled surface of my champagne. No.

They aren't even gnats:
the dreams of the elderly, memories
of the dead, as if
God had invented thought

from a handful of animated
punctuation marks.

They are a small lost crowd of tourists wandering
through the sad eternal

tourist trap of the past,
in search of some
trinket that might stand
for the pleasures they had

or failed to have. 1947. 1999. It all
ended at the mouth
of the falls, or the foot
of the mountain, or the ocean's edge, or in

the steady gaze of the embalmed
man in a coffin
at Ripley's Believe-It-Or-Not Museum.

Yes. The risen
joy and desperation
of the family vacation, all
that was felt and never said

turned to a fine black mist hovering
over the back
seat of a junkyard station wagon.

Or the wishes
of a fetus
floating in a jar.

Or so much bickering and love crossing
time zones
on a cell phone.

CONSOLATION

Winter birds, constant motion—

flight, fluster, or twitching in the trees. Early

afternoon, an old man with an appointment
arrives at the doctor's office hours too soon.

If only it could be seen
as some kind of prize.
Death. *Congrats! You did it: Life.*

No fish in the bowl.
The cat's asleep.
Today the quiet lull
of a bank holiday.

They come predictably enough, these
days without transaction. Other than that,
nothing much changes. On the roof

of the school, a dozen
white flags snap, and the children,
having just washed
their little hands, settle down for a snack.

Saltines, a piece of cheese, some
cool juice in a Dixie cup. Growing older, it is

one moment to the next in a simple passage.
Phase to phase. Blindfolded, walking

straight through one
immaterial mirror
and into another.
But it's never enough.

In the basement, there's a vault
full of raw material,
gleaming. How, without melodrama, can one

simply shrug that off?

And the music, and the terror, and those
Seven Wonders, and the prophecies, the novel
at the side of the bed:
how will that one end?

And the hush.
And the snow.
And the embezzlers, who will
be caught red-handed.

And the vanished, who will come back.

Hush.

Hush. The bankers are in their baths. The banks
are closed. And a dry
dust settles on the cash, and on the floor. Perhaps—

Perhaps there is a bridge, but that
bridge is underwater!

Yes. Of course. Just

because you never saw it
doesn't mean it wasn't there

all along, of course. Someone

always succumbs to the disease
the day before the cure is found.
Someone always shows up
with his properly filled-out forms
just as the doors are shut.

I would never have guessed.
I should have known.

For just a moment,
the birds pause in their commotion.

FOG

My ex-husband in the bulk food aisle
with an empty plastic bag, an infant
daughter, a blond son.
Wow. Hi. We hug. Plenty. Really. More than enough.

There is a kind of fog that rises only so high. Some
mornings, if you lie down on the lawn, it makes

a perfect shroud. Some mornings, if you sit
with your back against the picket fence, it
makes a nice shawl. True, too, that if

you put your ear to the center
of a soufflé, you can hear
the wind in there, no

longer desiring, not
the least bit dangerous.
Works just as well with a paper plate.

And the river, all this time, the river
has been rolling on and on, carrying
with it the infinite
scraps of silver lamé
that every river snatches
from the baggage of the desperate as it passes. Look:

Over there, two spectres,
unable to hold one another,
try to dance a sad waltz,

while, over there, two shadows ludicrously attempt
to strangle each other against a wall.
And here, here

in the bulk food aisle, I find
myself suddenly come to gather

ghostly figs, the sweet
weightless figs of amnesia, the pale
wasted figs of the gods—

gathering them shamelessly, grabbing them, tossing
        them,
tossing

them all
by fistfuls and handfuls
into a basket, a basket
with no bottom, a basket
weaved of imaginary straw

and manure and moss—and you, you

with your clear flimsy bag—harmless,
a lie, a small lie, a lie
told simply out of kindness. *Such*

a surprise! Christ,
so many years
of gathering and laughter—and fairly

decent intentions,
and pretty good times,
and this warm hug after, and still

you could be walking straight through me without a
        shiver
and I could be strolling across your grave with a smile.

TWO GIRLS

And so we began our stroll together down the path of
woe: afraid

when there was nothing to fear
and inflated with bravery when we should have been
        afraid.

All that scattered candy in the grass—those
were the hardest brightest flowers
of spring

but they bloomed without thinking beside the others,
        the ones
that emerged from the underworld
each year, bearing their sugary torches
as a warning.

The air was sweaty as petals.
We hated everyone
except ourselves. Or each other. Love, it was
a cool breeze at the center of a snow-globe. And, in it,
        a small
Alpine village, a steeple, and a stork. Swift
streams rolled
down the side of a mountain of laundry, tossing
two short skirts on the surface
of the water, skirts
made of foil.

Yes, our mothers
wept at the edge of that mountain
among the gloves and socks
and all the other strange, exhausting mysteries of loss.

But we were two girls
walking, walking
along the woeful path together
wearing our own flesh like
so much blood-soaked cake

while the guy who wanted to give us a ride
idled behind us
and the clouds ascended and descended from the sky's

purple burning like a tiered fountain.

Above us, a lot of fluff.

Not even a hint
of all the muffled suffering under it. So

why, already, was it the path of woe? Or was it?

ILLINOIS

We are up to our waists in the bloody
grass of it, not yet dead or divorced.
We are driving ourselves through the tarry
artery. You've read this poem before.

An atom smasher, an art museum,
A Styrofoam factory, a meatpacking plant.
A lot of blood on a lot of hands.

A bloody woman at the side of the road.
A bloody child in a bloody stroller.
Blood in our bodies. Blood in vats.
Blood in our hair. Blood on our hats.

If I give you the landfill, the apple orchard's mine.
If you give me the trailer court, the car lot's yours.

Again, it is that poem. The one in which the kids
who cannot see the future
find themselves in its accident. Today

there's a strange cloud pasted about the freeway.
A great static gray.

If we didn't know it was pollution, we'd gasp
and say, How beautiful!

We'd say, There *is* no future. Just
a freeway cut through someone else's state

a fast car on it
without brakes

this spine connected
briefly to this brain.

But lovers do not like to think.
They do not like to work.
The strippers do not like to swirl and stoop.
The lawyers can no longer bear to lie. The drunken

surgeon slips with his knife.

You are a husband.
I am a wife.
I'll nag. You drive.

You are a drummer,
and I am a waitress.
I am a servant,
you are a slave.

We are sloppy at our jobs
but so are they, so are they.
The weatherman is always
as honest as he is vague.

MESSAGE

On the other side of a wall
made of circuits and switches,
I hear my brother's wife whisper, *It's
her again. Let the machine get it.*

But you were the one I wanted, Machine.
You with your little, replaceable parts—
some of them fingers, some of them hearts.
This is a message for you:

It was late, I was lonely, again
I couldn't sleep. Briefly I remembered being

someone's little sister. A basketful of apples, fancy
cellophane crackling.

And then I got old
and ugly
and took to drink.

Machine, there is a wolf
full of meaning in my house. She

crouches in the corner. Unseasonably
warm, something
has crawled in on the fur-wet wind, and through
the wire and tin, I hear you humming. You

and your communion of immutable beings

breathing cleanly and listening to me.

FIRST HUSBAND

So where did they go, those
children we never had? Some

nights eyes shine and glow worms glow in ditches.
Perhaps a little girl emerges looking for her parents,
         worms
and thistles in her fists.

But you and I both know how
for years those children lived
off our bitter kisses—nothing

to eat in the house but hatred, love, and hope, al-
though

so many summers there was more
fruit than we could bear. A million

ripe tomatoes. The loam

porous as babies' breath
and old ankle bones.

Yes, yes, we spent

so many summers in that braggart's garden
deciding what to waste
and what to own
while our children starved
at home, inventing the machinery of snow.

MY FACE OUT THERE ON A CLOUD

Somewhere tonight there must be a man
who vaguely remembers me.

A blind owl blinks in a tree.

I'm glad. I am glad. May he remember me.

The plate is already dry, but I
make small circles at the center of it with a cloth.

August, already, and ten o'clock.
I stare dreamily into the dark back yard.

Out there, it's so dark
for a while I forget who I am.
I'm driving again
into the desert at night
as if it's a big black box.
The dashboard is an altar

strewn with maps and dust.

I see a woman at the side of the road, walking
into the middle of nothing. Oh
my God, I know
something suddenly.

I have eaten the fruit of knowledge.

I drop the cloth.

I have sipped from the cup of the subconscious.

My face out there on a cloud.

I know something now.
I hang the cloth on a hook on the back of a closet,
close it, and am gone.

EIGHTEEN DAYS OF RAIN
July/August 2000

The rain in the gutter sings the kind of song
women sing when they're falling out of love.

Or the kind of song I sang to my mother
her last night on the Oncology Ward.

Rain, certainly, but *eighteen days?*

Death, of course, but why this way?

At the end of it, the Bible says, God
sends a pastel cliché,
a brilliant bit of kitsch:
Something to piss off the cynics, or for
little girls to decorate their bedspreads with, this

symbol for cheerfulness, a pot of gold at the end of it
like God's big fist.

Thank you, Jesus. Thank you, God. Thank you, Holy
        Spirit.

But do you remember how she wept?

For half an hour they had
to tap the back of her hand
until one last vein that hadn't

already been wrecked could be had.
And then

those long last days. A creature
with wings pulling her under
then dragging her back to the surface. God? Remember,

when she wasn't drowning in her own lungs
we played a game of cards?

Hey, are you up there,
behind those weighty clouds? Are you
holding a sparrow
gently in your hand,
plucking the feathers from it one by one?

Forgive me, I didn't mean
for this to turn into
another protest song:

There have been other bodies,
other waters.
Please don't think
that I've forgotten.
Once, I lay

at the edge of one
with my hair spread out on the sand
while the sea tried to enter me
and behind me, on a blanket, a naked boy played
"Blowin' in the Wind" on his guitar.

Then, I was young, I thought
I *was* God, thought
silence
was a prayer.
And certainly, Lord, some nights,
listening to my own heart in the dark

what I still hear is his blond dog
chasing a stick into the warm waves there.

MRS. OLIVER
or, On a Wedding Anniversary

She wasn't entirely mortal, but he was.
Old song.
The refrain is easy to remember, it goes:

Love, love, what
the hell do you want from me?

She lived to see
vultures rip him to pieces in the street
then hang his flesh in the branches of the trees.

Oh, bandanas, bloody hankies, red silk scarves.

But, for the immortal, life goes on
and on and on and on.
Ten thousand Greek soldiers
marching to the sea.
The coronation of Anne Boleyn.
Freud, staring out the window, chewing on his pen.

Change never sleeps, though

winter remains the first season, and it's always another
        beautiful day
to be an opium-eater.

By the time I finally met her
it was 1973, and she

had become my sixth-grade teacher.
Overweight, widowed, divorced, divorced again, she
      had

a million facts she'd been
saving up for us. None of which

we would remember, only
the sense that love
could wreck our lives if we let it, that
nothing moved slower than time, and that

we could hold our breath as long as we liked

but we would never die.

RABBIT HOLE

Not a hole you could live in. Not

a hole you could use to climb into
or out of any trouble at all. For

a long time I thought
I was the only one. The only
one this beautiful, the only one who'd ever been

so madly in love I could die. Then, I got old.

Truly, I got old. I saw a girl today who was

the girl I was. Head thrown back in laughter. She
          didn't
see me, and never dreamt . . .

Full of love, made of lies. The lies
were like a lot of shiny pins
sticking the self that wasn't me
to the one I could have been. That

pinned-self, it used to make
a thin whisper as I walked, rustle
its see-through taffeta in the breeze. It smelled

like ether, and didn't bleed. That

rabbit freezes, smelling me—its
blank eye wide. Finally

it hurries into
a narrow hole in the snow, a place
where it's no less cold. But no noise.
A sense that there's a sun, but that it's far away—

light weakened
by the effort of shining, like

light shining through lingerie.

THE SECOND WEEK OF MAY

What will we buy with Judas's money?
Who will live in Hitler's house? What

shall we do with this veil stolen

from the murdered bride, this
blanket lifted from the sleeping child?

I will buy candy, says the sweetheart.
I will grow here, the primrose sings.

The lightness of silk in a perfumed breeze, soft
as cashmere, pale pink.

Where can we build
the house of spring,

the one built
on a clear conscience, the one
in which no innocent

civilian has ever been killed?
Yes. Imagine.
Every day
a clean kitchen, every night a Puritan's pillow.

But it's May, and the lilac
whispers to the wisteria,
Whose shadow shall I wear
this year to the prom? Whose

white scarf sewn from a virgin's last breath is this?

THE INTERNET

The first time I sit down to it alone
I am flesh surrounded by space.

The space begins at the edges of my body
and from there it expands to contain

everything.

I've sinned.
Cannot be saved.
Surrounding me is this strange haze
made of information.

There are owls trapped in barns
on fire. Hysterical with wings.
There are statues dumped
into the sea, the sea is full of these.

There are things I've said and done that still belong to me.
And the silence

in which they're packaged
accumulates like time, while through the window I see
a crane skid to a halt on the pond:
He was a child. Surely
he went to heaven.
It's been years since that boy died.
What makes me think I could speak to him now?

FOREST

There's a small one in my brain

beyond the tiny house, the lawn
mown by the miniature mower, the mall
and its matchbox cars parked in the little lot.

There's also an ocean
no bigger than the opal
my mother once wore on her left hand. At night

the fish still nibble
the flesh of her fingers in it. And a casino

the size of a sequin.
And a cathedral, like a seed.

But it's the forest that waits for me.

How many times in my life
have I wished to be alone?

The other children were throwing

sand on the beach. The elderly
aunt wanted
me to sit on her lap. Someone

humming in the library, the elevator.
The check-out line. The sidewalk sale. The tourists

leaning over the railing
to get a closer look at the falls, climbing
the stairs behind me
to the top of the Eiffel Tower.

Midnight, the baby cries.

The phone. The same
friend with her
same broken heart in Saskatchewan.

The Greyhound. The party. The kiss. The man

in the waiting room who wanted
to tell me about his cyst.

In that forest, I will.

Classroom strangely empty. Children grown.
No one's come to see
this particular movie but me. Not

another pair of headlights
on the highway, not
only for miles, for good.

It's a small forest, but the only path through it

ends where it began. It waits

at the edge of the rest of it for me

saving up names and phrases
I won't be needing again.

ZEUS

All night I ride my motorcycle up
and down the dirt
road between your house and town. Just

as sleep's about to slip
its loose white sack
over your nose and mouth, I'm
back, kicking
up the gravel with my tires—for

I am dust and sound, and nobody
fucks with dust, and silence
has a price. I

have a long grey ponytail
and a jacket
with *Meet Your Maker* embroidered on the back.

For now, you can't quite fathom that, though

you think hard, late at night, when
sleep won't come, and know
in the empty notebook
of your heart that

where thought ends, there's God. And

you're no longer young. The night

sky's a big mouth, opened wide. At least
two times you would have died
if it hadn't been for my rough kindness. That
time in Vegas with the gun, and

what was that other one? Passes

understanding, doesn't it? Or

maybe I'm just out here having fun. Maybe

if you lived on a little lake, I'd
ride my jet ski on it every night. I'd

wear a Hawaiian shirt, and I'd
be young and blond.
In any case, sleep will come
soon enough. Tonight

you can lie awake in the dark
and thank your lucky stars
that I chose your dirt road
to ride my motorcycle on.

WHY

He learns to say it, and for a while
there's nothing else to say, and not
an answer in this world to give him—in this world,
　　which is

a dish floating in a dreamed sea, circled
by a sun made of butter. The sugar

disperses sweetly in the breeze. Salt
is plentiful and cheap. Flour is lighter
and drier than snow, but until

you've tasted each, from a distance, as a vision—

Galileo. Columbus. The screams

of sailors on a ship
as it tips off the edge of the world
into an abyss
made of clarity, and more abyss.
He doesn't listen. He's only three. To him

it's obvious, and inexplicable. To me . . .

Twilight, the shadow of smoke.

Dawn, with its soft
and mismatched towels. The dog
chewing at its leash, the way
the fish are unimpressed
by the wind, which
has shifted everything from west to east

then back again in our sleep. How deep

the roots of weeds! How empty

the mirror—shining, industrious, clean. I
question my reflection in it,

but it looks blankly back at me, having

forgotten completely it once believed,
desperately, there was a reason.

"TODAY, A THIEF WHO STOLE BEE-HIVES, HANGED"
Excerpt from A Hangman's Diary: October 12, 15—

My son with his arms raised above him
in a wheatfield
in October

is a bit of folk art.

His eyes are made from bottle-caps.
Straw, his hair, and rubber bands.

But I have left the shadow
of my hand upon his making.
A scrap of breath and ghost.
A cold slow planet passes over.

In Nuremberg, Durer
is sketching a study for Christ's robe,
or two beautiful hands folded, while

on the bridge outside his window

the hangman waits with his rope.

VALENTINE

What was love to my mother before she was my mother?
Something scarlet

in the cage of doves, just
a glass of burgundy splashed

on a pale tablecloth, blood stain on the white carpet, a
      red

bra worn
under a sheer silk blouse. Oh,

I hadn't even been born, but I

was determined to make her a mother. I pulled

a needle and a thin red thread
smoothly through her, like a vein

and on the satin side of my mother's heart

I embroidered, *Be Mine*

and on the black lace, my name.

CREATION

Started with a plague of ladybugs one summer. So

much charm and destruction at once, a violent

funnel of humming and love. Once

I saw it myself on the horizon:
shiny, rising, a cloud of blood.
I was whistling *The Tennessee Stud*

while hunting for the frisbee of my son. I'd just

tossed a moldy arrangement of roses
into the dumpster
when a dead mole in the daisies and the sun
made me scream at the top of my lungs.

Flowers in the garbage.
Death in the garden.
Something new had started.
And I saw the new
thing with my own eyes, but then

that mole
wrenched itself
out of its own death to run. Has

any woman ever stood there, stunned
in her own silence for so long? It was

as if my scream had been a bolt
of lightning striking mud:
Suddenly, something
out of nothing.
Life had begun.

MACARONI & CHEESE

One day you may be asked, "How
was it that God brought forth
being

out of nothing?" Then, "Is
there no difference between them—
nothing, and being?" Outside

a strange slow snow, and a big
black bird hunched
over something in the road. The sky

will be a pale

reflection of itself,
like a woman making dreamy circles
at the center of a dish with a cloth.

Love. Hunger. Other alchemies.
You may be asked, "What

are my eyes made of? Can
Santa's reindeer be burned by fire? In
heaven, does Jesus eat?"
In the oven, something breathing. Rising. Melting.
        Shifting
shape and sweetening
in the heat. Now

you can see that the bird in the street
is wrestling something bloody

out of a carcass, trying
to expose its heart. You

put the dish down beside the cloth, and say,
"Darling, I don't know."

WORLD PEACE

A day like a mayfly on which someone slammed a
        Bible, all

exoskeletal radiance and insignificance in the dark. We
        find

ourselves the only
mother and child
who decided it was wise in this storm-impending crisis

to come to the County Fair.

Sheep among strangers. One
lone pony tethered to a pole. The prize
pig speaks eloquently in his sleep
on the tired subject of world peace, and the devil

who owns all this fairness outright
sits in a chair over there
by the fence
and lets his dog sniff around at the air. Briefly

it's air
made from the kind of paper
the repo-men roll through the halls of the house
to keep the mud on their boots from ruining your rugs
on the day they stomp
in and out
with all the things you ever bought on credit,
which, in the end, was everything you had:

As my grandma used to say,
We're going to have some weather.

But, at the moment, like petals—
a soft spray of spit, we are made of it.
And love, that slut, just

runs around deep-kissing everyone. So why

are we blind
to her wild suppositions
ninety-nine percent of the time?

Or does love generally never love us quite this much?

Well, might it suffice to say today I am struck dumb
by the laughable notion of numbers,

the whole hilarious idea of *greed?*
And the absurdity of feeling anything but peace
flies right over my head
like a flock of alarm clocks on the breeze.

Yes, Grandma, *God rest your soul,* we
will definitely have some weather,

but, for now,
the rides are quiet, the fun house is free, there are
no lines,

and at every gate a patient man or woman waits
for our tickets
with an open hand and a smile.

ACKNOWLEDGMENTS

Thanks to the following magazines, in which some of these poems first appeared:

American Poetry Review: "Clock Radio," "Hardware Store in a Town Without Men."

Crazyhorse: "First Husband."

The Cream City Review: "Message."

Fence: "Younger Woman Shopping for a Blouse."

The Iowa Review: "The Sorrows of Carrie M.," "Zeus."

The Kenyon Review: "Summer, Here," "Inscriptions on Wax Tablets."

New England Review: "Black Dress."

Witness: "Fortieth Birthday."